A Look at Germany

by Helen Frost

Consulting Editor: Gail Saunders-Smith, Ph.D.

Consultant: Hannelore Koehler
Information Officer
German Information Center, New York

Pebble Books

an imprint of Capstone Press
Mankato, Minnesota

Pebble Books are published by Capstone Press
151 Good Counsel Drive, P.O. Box 669, Mankato, Minnesota 56002
http://www.capstone-press.com

1 2 3 4 5 6 07 06 05 04 03 02

Library of Congress Cataloging-in-Publication Data
Frost, Helen, 1949–
  A look at Germany / by Helen Frost.
  p. cm.—(Our world)
  Summary: Simple text and photographs depict the land, animals, and
people of Germany.
  Includes bibliographical references and index.
  ISBN 0-7368-1430-2 (hardcover)
  ISBN 0-7368-9392-X (paperback)
  1. Germany—Juvenile literature. [1. Germany.] I. Title. II. Series.
DD17 .F76 2003
943—dc21   2001007795

Note to Parents and Teachers

The Our World series supports national social studies standards
related to culture. This book describes and illustrates the land,
animals, and people of Germany. The images support early readers
in understanding the text. The repetition of words and phrases
helps early readers learn new words. This book also introduces
early readers to subject-specific vocabulary words, which are
defined in the Words to Know section. Early readers may need
assistance to read some words and to use the Table of Contents,
Words to Know, Read More, Internet Sites, and Index/Word List
sections of the book.

Table of Contents

Berlin
★

Germany

N
W ← → E
S

Germany is a country
in the middle of Europe.
Germany is the fourth
largest country in Europe.
The capital of Germany
is Berlin.

Germany's flag

forest

plains

hills

mountains

6

Germany has forests, plains, hills, and mountains. Germany is warm in the summer. It is cold in the winter.

deer

beaver

8

Deer and foxes live
in Germany's forests.
Beavers and fish swim
in Germany's rivers.

More than 82 million
people live in Germany.
Most Germans live in towns
and cities. People in Germany
speak the German language.

Germans enjoy bread, cheese, and sausages. They also eat vegetables, pasta, and cake.

Many Germans enjoy
being outdoors. They
ride bicycles, ski, and swim.
Soccer is a popular sport
in Germany.

German workers make cars, electronics, and machines to earn money. Many Germans work in hotels, restaurants, and stores.

Germany's money is counted in euros.

Many Germans travel on fast trains between cities. They also travel on boats and airplanes. Most Germans drive cars.

Clockmakers in Germany's Black Forest make cuckoo clocks. The Black Forest has pine trees and waterfalls.

Words to Know

capital—the city in a country where the government is based; Berlin is the capital of Germany; about 3.5 million people live in Berlin.

cuckoo clock—a clock shaped like a small house; a wooden bird pops out of the clock every hour and makes the sound "cuckoo."

Europe—one of the seven continents of the world

language—the words and grammar that people use to talk and write to each other

sausage—a kind of cooked meat that has spices, herbs, and salt

soccer—a game played by two teams of 11 players; players try to score by kicking a ball into a goal at each end of a field; soccer is called "Fussball" in Germany.

waterfall—a place where river water falls from a high place to a lower place

Read More

Alcraft, Rob. *Germany.* A Visit To. Des Plaines, Ill.: Heinemann Library, 1999.

Frank, Nicole, and Richard Lord. *Welcome to Germany.* Welcome to My Country. Milwaukee: Gareth Stevens, 2000.

Gray, Shirley W. *Germany.* First Reports. Minneapolis: Compass Point Books, 2002.

Internet Sites

German Flag Quiz/Printout
http://www.EnchantedLearning.com/europe/germany/flag/flagquizbw.shtml

Germany Geography
http://www.photius.com/wfb2000/countries/germany/germany_geography.html

Welcome to Germany Info
http://www.germany-info.org

Index/Word List

beavers, 9
Berlin, 5
bicycles, 15
Black Forest, 21
cars, 17, 19
cheese, 13
cities, 11, 19
cuckoo clocks,
  21

deer, 9
Europe, 5
fish, 9
forests, 7, 9
hills, 7
language, 11
live, 9, 11
money, 17
mountains, 7

plains, 7
restaurants, 17
rivers, 9
sausages, 13
sport, 15
swim, 9, 15
trains, 19
waterfalls, 21
workers, 17

Word Count: 162
Early-Intervention Level: 17

Editorial Credits

Mari C. Schuh, editor; Kia Adams, series designer; Jennifer Schonborn and
  Patrick D. Dentinger, book designers; Alta Schaffer, photo researcher

Photo Credits

Blaine Harrington III, 14
Capstone Press/Gary Sundermeyer, 12
Corbis/Bob Krist, 20
Courtesy of German Information Center, New York, 16
Flat Earth Collection, 1
Fritz Polking/Visuals Unlimited, 6 (bottom right)
Index Stock Imagery/Everett Johnson, 6 (bottom left); Elfi Kluck, 8 (top); Canstock
  Images Inc., 8 (bottom)
International Stock/Tom & Michele Grimm, cover
J.C. Carton/Bruce Coleman, Inc., 17 (bill)
One Mile Up, Inc., 5
Reuters/HO/Archive Photos, 17 (coin)
TRIP/B. Gadsby, 6 (top right); M. Barlow, 10; B. Turner, 18
Unicorn Stock Photos/Aneal E. Vohra, 6 (top left)